C000226064

Whatever Happened to the Brethren?

A survey of local churches in 1998-99

Partnership

A service for local churches
Registered Office: 23 Percy Road, London N21 2JA
Web: www.partnershipuk.org Registered Charity No: 802564

Whatever Happened to the Brethren?

A survey of local churches in 1998-99

Graham Brown

Published for

by

PATERNOSTER PRESS

First published 2003 by Partnership and Paternoster Press

09 08 07 06 05 04 03   7 6 5 4 3 2 1

British Library Cataloguing in Publication Data
A catalogue record for this book is available from the British Library.

ISBN 0-900128-24-0

Cover design by Paulo Baigent.
Typeset by Profile, Culmdale, Rewe, Exeter.
Produced by Jeremy Mudditt Publishing Services, Carlisle,
and published by Partnership and Paternoster Press,
PO Box 300, Carlisle, Cumbria CA3 0QS.
Printed and bound in Great Britain
by Bell and Bain Ltd, Glasgow.

Contents

PREFACE

Neil Summerton

Partnership's predecessor body, The Christian Brethren Research Fellowship (CBRF), was true to its appellation in that, during the 25 years of its existence, it promoted a wide range of research into the life and activities of the 'Open' wing of the Brethren movement in the British Isles. Much of this was historical, and that endeavour is now carried forward by the Brethren Archivists and Historians Network under the able leadership of Neil Dickson. One aspect of the research was, however, statistical. It was an effort to provide up-to-date factual information on the position of the churches of the Open connexion. The purpose was to inform thinking and action by the leaderships of this type of local church, and by the bodies which support them in various ways. The hope was to reduce dependence on perceptions, assumptions and hunches alone.

The work began with a survey of 75 churches in 1966[1]. It was orientated towards evangelism, and perhaps reflected wider Evangelical concerns at the time about evangelistic effectiveness and methods.[2] It was followed in 1978 by a wider survey[3] to which 249 churches responded; while the evangelistic concerns of the 1966 were pursued, a larger number of questions were asked and in particular an effort was made to explore attitudes

---

1   Graham D Brown, 'How can we improve our evangelism? Deductions from a survey of assemblies' in *The Journal of the Christian Brethren Research Fellowship*, no. 31, May 1971.
2   See Ian Randall and David Hilborn, *One Body in Christ: The History and Significance of the Evangelical Alliance*, Carlisle: The Paternoster Press, 2001, pp. 270 -275; and *On the other side: The Report of the Evangelical Alliance's Commission on Evangelism*, London: Scripture Union for the Evangelical Alliance, 1968, and the associated statistical report referred to at appendix A in the report.
3   Graham Brown and Brian Mills, *'The Brethren' today: a factual survey*, Exeter: The Paternoster Press for the Christian Brethren Research Fellowship, 1980.

on matters known to be of critical concern in the churches at the time. This last objective produced somewhat problematical results and, when Partnership undertook a further survey in 1988, it chose to confine itself to the more factual aspects of the two earlier surveys. The opportunity was however taken to draw on data collected at more or less the same time by MARC Europe in its English Church Attendance survey. These reinforced the data from the Partnership survey, and strengthened it in that a considerable number of local churches responded to MARC Europe, who had not responded to the Partnership questionnaire. A consolidated report was published in 1993.[4]

In view of the earlier surveys and of the rapidly changing position in the churches with which Partnership is in touch, a further survey was made in the winter of 1998-99. In this case, it was decided to keep the questionnaire close to that used in 1988, precisely in order to permit comparisons between 1998 and 1988, and, where possible, even with the information for 1978 and 1966. It is the results of the 1998-99 survey which are being presented in this volume.

The four surveys, together with the information from the English Church Attendance survey of 1989, provide an invaluable body of information, for three reasons.

First, they are a comparatively rare example of what the social researchers call 'longitudinal' data. That is, they permit this group of churches to be viewed through a series of snapshots, taken from broadly the same vantage point, over time. In particular, they permit change to be observed with a measure of precision.

That leads to the second reason. The surveys have been taken during a deeply sensitive period in the evolution of this group of churches. It has been a period of rapid decline, haemorrhaging of leadership and others to other church groupings, soul-searching, crisis of identity, and pressure from the emergence of new church groupings with, in many respects, a similar ethos. The self-sufficient confidence and sense of divine appointment which this group of churches possessed up to the mid-1960s quickly collapsed in the face of these pressures. These longitu-

---

4   Peter Brierley, Graham Brown *et al.*, *The Christian Brethren as the Nineties began*, Carlisle: The Paternoster Press for Partnership in association with MARC Europe, 1993.

dinal data permit us to observe the processes, and the responses that the churches have been making, with a degree of detail and precision. In the midst of the period an important conference asked the question, 'Where do we go from here?' In some respects, at least, the results of the 1998-99 survey, in comparison with those from the earlier surveys, indicate where the responding churches went! In short, the four surveys enable us to observe change in the subject churches.

The third reason why the results are valuable is that they enable individual church leaderships to compare their own congregation with the collective results for the members of the 'family' as a whole, and with the results for three main sub-groupings (the larger churches, medium-sized churches, and small churches). Because leaderships rightly have to concern themselves with the fortunes of their own churches, and have to commit themselves pretty well exclusively to them, often they have to rely on anecdotal evidence about what is happening in the 'family' more generally. Sometimes, indeed, they are better informed about developments in other church groupings (though there is no implication here that there is anything wrong with that). These data may help leaders of individual churches to see the 'family' and its recent development as a whole. They may indeed enable them to think better of the 'family' than they are sometimes inclined to do!

This is not the place to attempt to summarise the main results of the 1998-99 survey. A summary of the main findings immediately follows this introduction, in a convenient note form.

It may however be worth referring to a number of particular features of the results:

- The continuing sharp decline in the number of congregations of Open Brethren background in the United Kingdom. There has been a decline between a sixth and a fifth in the short period between 1990 and 1998, on top of the decline of about a further fifth that took place between 1959 (the peak year according to the conventional address lists) and 1990. In the thirty-eight years up to 1997, the address lists suggest a decline of some 30% in the number of congregations of Open Brethren background. The evidence of this latest survey is that, because of demographic structure and lack of conversions, the loss of smaller churches is likely to continue for some time yet. Despite the efforts of organisations like the

Church Planting Initiative, the rate of establishment of new congregations nothing like offsets the closure rate. (Of course, since it is generally small churches which close, the total number of individual members of churches of Brethren background has probably not fallen as dramatically as the number of congregations.)

- Nor, it should be noted, is the demise of small churches being offset by the growth of medium-sized and large churches. In this respect, the message of the survey should not be masked by the success of a limited number of large churches. In 1998-99 the great body of the churches surveyed were four or so members/regular attenders smaller than they were ten years before, on a median size of less than fifty. That is, most churches were 10% smaller than they were ten years earlier. Numerically, the Nineties were not a good decade for these churches.

- There are churches of all sizes, however, which buck this trend. In particular, there is a small group of larger churches which appeared to be forging ahead at the time of the survey. We would do well to note their character, activities and organisation, to see what lessons can be learned by other churches with similar roots. In Partnership, one of our prime aims is to disseminate information of that type among the churches, particularly among those which are members of Partnership. At the same time, we should note that the success of this group of larger churches is in considerable part attributable to their ability, in competition with other churches in their neighbourhoods, to attract Christians who are moving into those neighbourhoods. There is a question mark over the effectiveness even of the large churches in securing conversions on the scale being achieved by a few local churches at least in the UK. Here is a question which this group of churches needs to address – along with most churches in the UK: how can churches be more effective in evangelism, as distinct from attractiveness to those who already are Christians?

- This question is worth asking in the light of a further strong feature of this group of churches, as evidenced by the survey results. That is, their continuing impulse towards foreign mission. That is historically one of the clearest features of the Open Brethren movement. Chapter 10 indicates how strong that tradition remains.

A further key feature of the results is worth noting in conclusion. That is the question whether they do not indicate that the responding churches are breaking down into two broad groups: (1) smaller churches which retain the basic approaches and style which were characteristic of the Brethren movement for over a century; and (2) medium-sized and larger churches whose character and style has changed decisively over the period of these surveys, while maintaining a commitment to certain key ecclesiological insights of the movement. This raises the further question of how far it will be sensible to try to continue surveying churches of this background as if they comprise in any sense a composite whole. The differences between the two groups within the whole may shortly become so sharp that it makes no sense to try to analyse them as a single whole – that the resulting averages would be meaningless.

This is a question which Partnership can continue to ponder over the next few years, though I am confident that we shall during that period want to mount some surveys directed specifically to understanding the character and needs of Partnership churches better than we do at present.

Once again, the hearty thanks of Partnership are due to Graham Brown, who was largely responsible for designing the survey, who has done all the work of marshalling the responses and compiling the information from them, and who has been largely responsible for writing up the results. Without his commitment, there simply would have been no further stage in this longitudinal study of the evolution of churches of Open Brethren background. Indeed, the series of four surveys has been very much his achievement. All this has been done while being a key leader of a local church as well as until recently pursuing a career as a market researcher. Will volunteer understudies please line up in an orderly manner!

Neil Summerton

Methods and Significance

This study, like earlier ones at ten-yearly intervals, was carried out by means of a postal questionnaire. This was designed to be as close as possible to the questioning and structure of the 1988 study to enable comparisons to be made wherever possible.

Study Frame and Coverage

We set out to survey as many assemblies and churches of (Open) Brethren background as possible using as a frame a list produced in 1997[1] by Christian Year Publications. This was supplemented to cover those churches known to be of Brethren background, who for some reason or other do not appear in the list. The previous survey carried out in 1988 used a similar list published in 1983[2]. That list was scanned to see if there were churches which did not appear in the 1997 list, but which were known still to be in existence. The survey this time did not include churches in Northern Ireland; it was restricted to those in England, Wales and Scotland. It is worth noting that the coverage in Northern Ireland in 1988 was very slight.

In 1998, questionnaires were sent to 1117 churches. Replies were received from 344 churches. Of these replies 10 were from churches declining to complete the survey questionnaire and a further 12 were in respect of churches which had appeared on the 1997 list and which had since closed. Thus a total of 322 churches were included in the survey in 1998.

The response rate, allowing for the closed churches, was

---

1   *The Assemblies Address Book* (Fourth Edition) Bath: Christian Year Publications
2   *Christian Brethren Assemblies round the World*, Glasgow: Pickering and Inglis

therefore 29%. The comparable number of churches completing the study in 1988 was 308. The overall response rate for the whole of Great Britain is 29% – substantially higher than achieved in 1988. This is probably because of the omission of Northern Ireland, which had a low rate in 1988. This is a good response rate for a postal survey without a systematic reminder follow-up. The significance of the response rate and the associated data is discussed below.

Geographic Spread

The geographic spread of responses was wide. Table 1 shows the numbers responding and the % of the total number of churches on the list in that area. Together these provide a response rate by region.

Region	Responding	On List	%
London & South East	79	267	30%
Midlands	33	129	26%
East Anglia	24	58	41%
South West	59	182	32%
Wales	20	82	24%
North West	34	110	31%
Yorks + North East	13	61	21%
Scotland	60	228	26%
Total	322	1117	29%

Table 1: Response Rate by GB Region

The regional variance shown in 1998 runs from a low of 21% in Yorkshire and the North East to a high of 41% in East Anglia. Scotland and Wales too showed below average returns. The numbers involved do not however enable detailed comparisons by area, since the sample sizes are subject to wide statistical variance when comparing between regions.

The analysis focuses more, as in previous years, on the differences between various sizes of church. The difference in practice and behaviour is very marked between 'Small' churches (those with under 30 regular attenders) and those described as 'Large' (with 70 regular attenders or more). These differences will be covered as each subject area is examined and the effect of these Large churches on the growth and decline of the movement as a whole elucidated in the next chapter. It will be seen that there has been substantial development in these Large churches. The numbers of churches shown by size of congregation are recorded in Table 2. Just over a third of churches are under 30 in size, a further third being between 30 and under 70, while just under a quarter were at above 70. 6% of assemblies did not provide a figure for their size.

No of Members	Responding	%
1-29	114	35%
30-69	116	36%
70+	74	23%
Not Stated	18	6%
Total	322	100%

Table 2: Size of Churches responding

Studies like these need to be not only representative, but also reliable. The use of a postal questionnaire is quite common in this kind of study and the rate of questionnaires returned is quite good, judged by the standard of returns on commercial surveys. This is particularly so given the complexity of the survey and the fact that some research would be required by the person completing the questionnaire, in order to answer the questions on statistical growth and decline. Face-to-face interviewing is subject to its own biases and non-response in that kind of study is often as high if not higher than in postal surveys.

Whether the study can be regarded as representative of all Open Brethren churches is more difficult to ascertain, since there has been no follow-up of non-respondents to see if there is any difference between those who did respond and those who did not. It is clear that care must be taken in regarding these data as representative of the whole body of Open Brethren churches in

Great Britain. We recognise that it is possible that, given the identity of the organisers of the survey, the responses may over-represent the more progressive churches. What can be said with absolute certainty (subject to the point below about the reliability of the data in the responses) is that the responses give an accurate picture of the 322 responding churches. The data add to our understanding of this group of independent evangelical churches! They are particularly valuable in view of the opportunity to compare them with the data from the same group of churches in 1988, 1978 and even from the much smaller and narrower survey of 1966.

Then there is the question of reliability of data. Postal studies rely on the willingness of respondents to understand, complete and return the questionnaire. Comment is sometimes made on their lesser ability to provide reliable data since there is no one checking on the respondent's understanding of the questions nor of the validity of the answers, which a face-to-face interviewer might provide. Use of a postal questionnaire can be an advantage where data has to be sourced from several places. Face-to-face interviewing which requires a respondent to provide data straightaway, particularly when time constraints are involved can mean that respondents are led to guess answers sometimes. In any case, the cost and complexity of face-to-face work in a study like this makes it impractical.

We are grateful to all those who did respond. A detailed examination of the questionnaires indicates that much thought had gone into providing answers and information. A number of respondents indicated that the exercise provided a useful review of their church life and was worthwhile for that alone. It is to be hoped that the learning provided from an examination of the overall picture will prove similarly instructive.

Pen-picture of 322 Responding Churches in 1998-9

The Average Brethren Church. . .

- Has 58 members/attenders
- Has been increasing in size by 2% a year recently
- Has had 5 conversions and 4 baptisms in the past two years
- Centres its worship around the Breaking of Bread service
- Allows women to take some part in services
- Focuses evangelism on family services and youth activities
- Is led by a team of elders

Churches are changing. . .

- Larger churches are growing
  - *14 churches have over 200 members/attendees*
- Growth has come from both conversions and transfer growth
  - *Both medium and large churches show a 3% growth from conversions*
- Only 6% of churches reported no conversions
  - *But 27% would not state a number*
- Family services are now held in 75% of churches vs 46% ten years ago
- 53% allow women to take part (audibly) in services
  - *In 21% of small churches vs 83% of large churches*
- 33% of churches have at least one full- or part-time resident worker
  - *45% of churches plan to have one in place within two years*

The Average Large Church of 70+ members . . .

- Has 116 members/attenders

- Has been increasing by 5% in the last two years
  - *Transfer growth is mainly from non-Brethren churches*
- Has an age profile close to the total GB population
- Has had 10 conversions and 8 baptisms in the past two years
- Tends to centre its worship around a Sunday morning event
- Focuses evangelism on family services, youth activities and seeker Bible studies
- Allows women to take part audibly in services
- Offers a wide range of activities
- Has a full-or part-time resident worker (69%)

The Average Small Church of under 30 members . . .

- Has 17/members/attenders
- Has been decreasing by 3% in the last two years
  - *Mainly through deaths of members*
  - *Gets transfer growth from other Brethren churches*
- Has an age-profile markedly skewed to the elderly
- Has had 2 conversions and 1 baptism in the past two years
- Centres its worship around the Breaking of Bread service on Sunday mornings
- Does not allow women to take audible part in services
- Focuses evangelism on gospel meetings on Sunday evenings
- Cannot offer a wide range of activities but often tries to
- Does not have a full- or part-time worker and does not plan to get one.

Size and Trends from the 1998 Survey

The Overall Picture

Numbers of Churches

The survey took as its starting point the list of local churches in Great Britain published in 1997 by Christian Year Publications. Just over 1100 churches from England, Scotland and Wales were listed in that publication. To this were added a handful which were recognised as having 'Brethren roots'. This gave a total of 1117 in all. A questionnaire was sent to each of these. (The questionnaire is reproduced as an Appendix.) From returns received it appears that 11 in England had closed down leaving a total of 1106. These 1106 churches were split between the three countries as shown in Table 3, which also provides figures from the same source in 1990 (thus allowing a comparison on the overall number of listed congregations in the two years).

	1998	1990	% 98/90
England	796	977	-17
Scotland	228	277	-18
Wales	82	102	-20
GB	1106	1356	-18

Table 3: Number of Churches by Country

Since 1990 there has been a drop of around 18% in the number of local churches of this type across the whole country, the decline being fairly evenly spread between England, Scotland and Wales. This is on top of a drop in the number of 19% in the period 1959 to 1990. Overall, from the peak number of 1551 in 1959, Open Brethren congregations in Britain have dropped by 29% (though Open Brethren numbers have declined less markedly).

Size of Churches

The first question in the survey asked about the size of the responding congregation, defining this as either the number in fellowship or membership, or the number of Christians who attended regularly at the time of response.

	Average Number	**% growth**
1978	52	
1988	52	0
1998	58	12

Table 4: Average Size of Churches 1978 vs 1988 vs 1998

Table 4 shows that the average size of churches responding to either of these definitions was 58. This shows an increase from the 1988 figure of 52, which compares with a similar figure of 52 in 1978. This seems to indicate a growth over the previous ten years of at least 12% within the churches which are remaining. This is a heartening trend in days when church attendances are in decline across all denominations. However before too many conclusions are drawn from the data about a resurgence of growth in the movement as a whole it is worth looking at the survey returns in more detail.

What is an 'Average Church'?

The figures given above are described as mean averages. That is, they are calculated by taking the size of each church and adding them all up to give a grand total, which is then divided by the number of churches responding. It is a commonly used measure

of an average. This is what one would do if calculating bats-
men's averages at cricket. However it is not the only way of
looking at averaging data. Sometimes the median – or 'middle-
sized' unit of a range of numbers gives a more accurate reflec-
tion of what is happening within a group.[1]

If then we look at the median or middle-sized churches in the
1988 and 1998 surveys (see Table 5), we find that in fact the
median measure declined from 47 in 1988 to 43 in 1998 – a drop
of 4 members. This is in contrast to the increase of 6 using the
mean average figure.

	Mean Average No of Members	Median Average No of Members
1978 vs 1988 vs 1998		
1978	52	
1988	52	47
1998	58	43

Table 5: Average Size of Churches

How then do we account for the disparity between the two
measures and what does it mean? Has the average church
increased in size or not? For this we need to look at the numbers
of churches by size of membership/attendance.

---

1 Suppose, for example, a group has ten members, each of whom has an
income per annum of ten thousand pounds. The mean average income
for the group is £10,000. The middle-sized or median average is the
same. If Bill Gates, the chairman of Microsoft, joins the group with his
annual income valued in millions of pounds, the mean average income
of the group will rise considerably, since his income will be averaged
across all the rest of the members. In fact, unless Bill Gates actually
gives his income to others in the group, the middle-sized or median
member will still have £10,000. The mean average would be arithmeti-
cally accurate, but it would be misleading if used to assess whether the
average person in the group was richer or not.

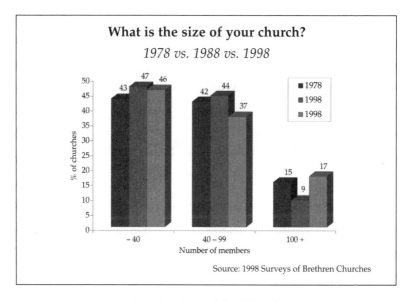

Chart 6: Size of the Church

Chart 6 shows the proportion of churches in three groups – those with under 40 members, those with 40 to 99 members, and those with 100 members or more. It will be seen that there is a big jump in the proportion of churches with more than 100 members/attendees.

If we look at the other end of the size scale, we do not see a big increase in the number of small churches, but the charting method and the width of the size groups chosen do not make it easy to detect whether churches here are growing smaller. What we can do is to look at the effect of polarisation of size on the make-up of churches replying to the survey.

The growth of the larger churches has affected the figures for average size.

If we look more closely at the details of church size in the data we see that there were in fact 14 churches which had more than 200 members in 1998. In 1988 there was only 1 of this size. These 14 churches account for about 18% of the number of members in churches replying to the survey.

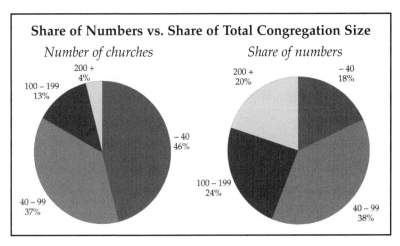

Chart 7: Share of Numbers vs Share of Congregation Size

Chart 7 shows the number of churches in each size range and breaks out those with 200+ separately. They account for 4% of the churches. However they also account for 20% of the total numbers attending. At the other end of the scale, churches under 40 in size account for 46% of the numbers of churches – almost half, but only 18% of the total numbers attend these churches. If we add in all churches over 100 in size, the largest churches account for 17% of the number of churches, but 44% of total attendance.

Average Size by Region

The average size by region is particularly affected by the presence of large churches. The figures by region are shown in Table 8.

	Mean Average	Median Average
Total GB	58	43
London, Southern and South East	52	46
South West and Wales	54	40
Midlands, East Anglia, Northern England	56	42
Scotland	74	49

Table 8: Average Size of Churches – By Region

The sample in Scotland included 7 churches with over 200 in size. This meant that the mean average church size in that region was 74, well above the national average of 58. Each of the remaining regions of GB were slightly below the national average figure. Looking at the median or middle-sized church average, both Scotland and the South East of England were above the national figure. Generally speaking, the congregations are significantly larger in these areas than in the others, particularly so in Scotland. Comparing the mean average with the median (or middle-sized) figures, the Scottish data in particular demonstrate how different a situation can seem when seen from a different perspective.

While data was collected for all parts of GB (but not Northern Ireland) the sample sizes are too small to make it worthwhile breaking out data for smaller areas. Variation in the data due to small sample size also makes it unwise to draw out trends from regional figures.

Growth and Decline

From the above it seems that while the number of churches declined by 18%, the numbers of attenders per church rose by 12%. The overall effect was a total reduction in attendance of 8%. This is another way of saying that it is the smallest churches which close. An estimate of the number of people associated with the movement may be obtained by multiplying the average size of churches by the total number appearing on the list.

(This assumes that non-responding churches have the same average size as those who did respond.) The numbers attending in total across GB by country is seen in Table 9.

	1998	**1990**	**% change**
England	44748	48850	-8
Scotland	16872	16066	+5
Wales	4035	3978	+1
GB	64786	70512	-8

Table 9: Numbers attending Brethren Churches in GB 1998 vs 1990

These figures are higher than those published by the UK Christian Handbook by a factor of some 25%. However both show similar downward movements over time. It is interesting to note that overall numbers do not seem to have declined in Wales and Scotland, the bulk of the fall coming in England – a finding which may itself reflect differences in overall religious practice between the three countries. Thus although numbers of churches have fallen, those that remain have been somewhat successful in picking up in size.

This ties in with some of the data which churches report on their own growth. The next chapter looks at how the individual churches perceived their progress.

Summary and Conclusions

The number of churches with Brethren roots has been in decline over the past years with the decline in the past decade continuing apace. The numbers attending the churches that remain – according to the survey – has shown an increase, if we look at the arithmetic or mean average. The result is that the total numbers of attenders has fallen by less than the number of churches. However it is the larger churches which have been growing – in particular the very large ones with over 200 members/attenders. This is a heartening finding, since it shows that decline is not inevitable. Much of the reported findings will examine what these larger churches are doing and the lessons which can be leaned from their experience. However there is no evidence that the decline in overall numbers of churches has been halted. As the next chapter shows the smaller churches are overwhelmingly elderly and have not been increasing in size. Many are obviously in terminal decline.

3

Growth and Decline in the 1998 Survey

For any particular local church, growth or decline can happen independently of what is happening to other churches around or the movement as a whole. Part of the survey asked about their perceptions of progress and then looked in detail at what lay behind the movements they observed

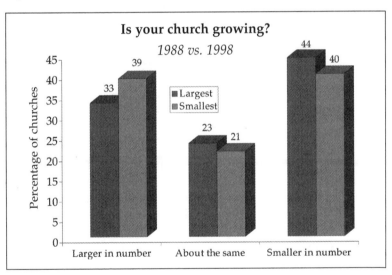

Chart 10: Description of Growth – 1988 vs 1998

Chart 10 shows their answers to the question 'Has the total number in membership increased or decreased over the past five years?' Nearly as many churches thought that they were growing as were showing decline. Over the decade, there was an increase in the number of those who reported larger attendances.

There was also a slight decrease in the percentage reporting a decline. It appears that it is relatively rare for churches to remain constant in size, that there is either progress and growth, or that numbers dwindle.

Which of the churches were growing and which declining?

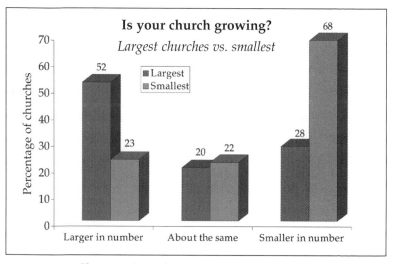

Chart 11 Growth – Large vs Small churches

Chart 11 shows that the larger churches were twice as likely to be showing growth as the smaller ones. These ratios are fairly similar to those reported in 1988. Large churches were more likely to be growing while smaller ones were more likely to be declining. However being large was not a precondition for growth. Only half of the larger churches showed growth. About a quarter showed decline while a further quarter were stable in size over the decade. Of the smaller churches about a quarter were growing, but over half showed a decline.

What are the factors behind the growth? Why are churches continuing to grow or decline?

Factors contributing to growth or decline

There are various ways of looking at growth and where it is coming from. Churches grow for a number of reasons. People move home and district and find a new church, or they become disillusioned with a church and move on to another in the same area. This process is called Transfer Growth. Growth also happens because some members have children who grow up and, in turn, become part of the church. A church may also lose members because of death. This is called Biological Growth. People also are converted and join a church, while others (negatively) drop out of the Christian scene. This is referred to as Conversion Growth. In the survey each church was asked to estimate how many people who had joined or left fell into each of the above-mentioned categories of growth. These data were then compared with the size of each church to arrive at a percentage rate of growth. Chart 12 looks at this % rate of growth over the previous two years as reported by each church and compares it with similar data ten years previously.

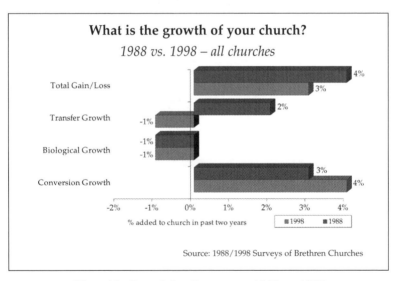

Chart 12: Growth by Category – 1988 vs 1998

The picture shown is that churches grew during the two years prior to the survey. The growth rate across all churches was 4% – slightly higher than ten years before when it was 3%. Looking at the detail of growth, conversion growth contributed 3% to the size of the church. More people were added to the church through conversion than dropped out. Transfer growth added another 2%, since the number joining from other churches, was higher than those leaving to join other churches. Biological growth was a negative –1%. In other words the number of people dying exceeded the number of the children of members, who joined the church, having come to faith themselves. These rates of growth are net figures. In other words they set off the losses against the gains in each category.

If each category of growth is examined in more detail it will be seen in Chart 13 that the gross rates of gain and loss show an interesting pattern.

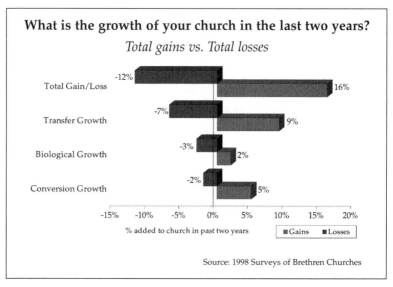

Chart 13: Growth by Category – Gains vs Losses

The average church grew overall by 16% gross in the two years up to 1998. This was offset by the 12% who for one reason or another left the church – they either moved, died or dropped out. Looking in more detail at the components of this 16%, inward transfer growth was the highest figure with +9% – that is, more than half the growth of the church came from people moving into the church from another church. At the same time –7% moved out in the same period. (It should be borne in mind that these figures comprise both people moving to another district and those who do not leave the district but move to another church for some reason.) Conversion growth at +5% was off-set by –2% who, it was thought, dropped out completely. These latter people did not move to any other church. Death account-ed for a decline of –3%, which was not entirely offset by the number of children of members coming into membership.

This information underlines the importance of maintaining a healthy inflow of people transferring into the church. If, for some reason this stops, the decline from 'transfers out', death and peo-ple dropping out can soon push the church into overall decline.

As might be expected growth rates differ according to the size of the church. Chart 14 shows the net growth rate by small, medium and large churches.

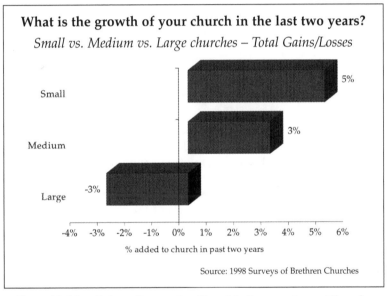

What is the growth of your church in the last two years?

Small vs. Medium vs. Large churches – Total Gains/Losses

% added to church in past two years

Source: 1998 Surveys of Brethren Churches

Chart 14: Net Gain or Loss – Small vs Medium vs Large Churches

While small churches declined by some -3% net, medium churches increased by +3% and large churches by +5%. It is instructive to look at the gross rate of increase and the gross decline by size.

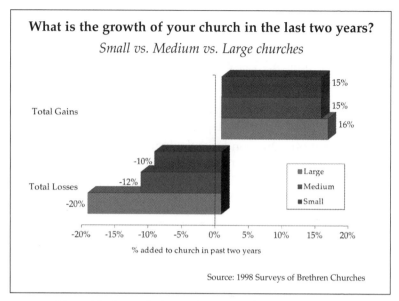

What is the growth of your church in the last two years?
Small vs. Medium vs. Large churches

Source: 1998 Surveys of Brethren Churches

Chart 15: Gross Gains and Losses – by Size of Church

All three categories by size had similar gross rates of gain. The small churches had higher losses – at a rate of –20% they had almost double the rates experienced by the larger churches. When the areas of growth for each category are examined, the reasons for this become clear. Chart 16 shows the net rates of growth for each type of growth across the three categories.

Biological Growth

Small churches have a high rate of loss in this category. The large churches were in balance while the medium sized group fell between the two. Small churches were affected by a high death rate, few births and few young people in the church. Chart 17 shows the age make-up of the churches in the various categories.

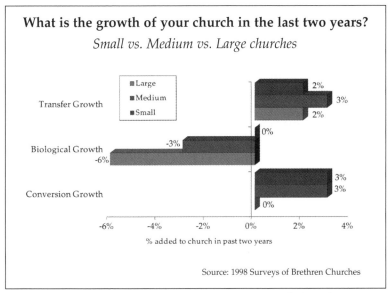

Chart 16: Growth by Category – by Size of Church

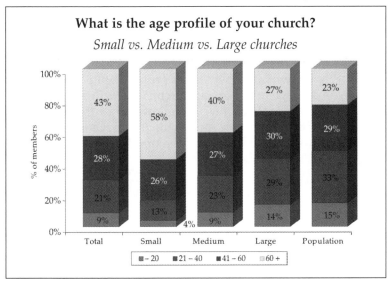

Chart 17: Age Profile by Size of Church

The average church had an ageing population, since it had nearly half of its members in the age group 60 years and over, against just 28% for that age-group in the population as a whole. The groups aged 40 and under were poorly represented, making up 30% of the church population as against 48% of the population at large. The largest churches most nearly matched the overall GB population. Small churches, however, had nearly 70% of their members in the 60+ age group, with only 17% under the age of 40.

Transfer Growth

The differing overall rates of growth of the churches were not affected by transfer growth, since in this category the net rates for all three sizes were alike, with the large churches, if anything, having a slightly lower rate. The argument that larger churches grow mainly by transfer growth – by 'sheep-stealing' – seems from these data to be unproven. Indeed the rate of gain from 'local' transfer growth for small churches (+6%) was higher than for the large churches (+3%). Again the medium churches were between the two.

Conversion Growth

For the large church, conversions seem to be more important. Indeed for conversion growth the large and medium churches matched one another with +3% net growth while there was no growth on average in the small churches. Growth by conversion and subsequent baptism into the fellowship of the church has been one of the important focuses of the movement over the years. The next chapter examines the trends in more detail.

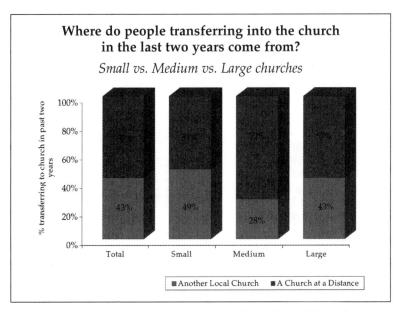

Where do people transferring into the church in the last two years come from?

Small vs. Medium vs. Large churches

Chart 18: Source of Transfer Growth by Size of Church

If we look in more detail at where the transfer growth is coming from, we see from Chart 18 that in the average church just over 43% of newcomers came from another church in the locality. Large churches were at this average level, while small churches were more likely to have a higher proportion – almost half – join from other local fellowships. Only in medium size churches does the figure fall to 28%, with the vast majority of 'transfers in' coming from churches at a distance.

So where are these new members transferring from – what sort of churches have they left? Chart 19 below shows the proportion who have come from Brethren churches.

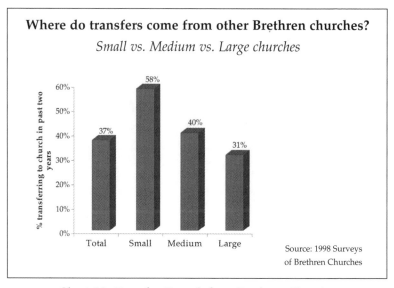

Chart 19: Transfer Growth from Brethren Churches

Less than 40% of new members transferring into the responding churches in the previous two years came from other
Brethren churches. In small churches the figure was a sizeable
58%, while in medium-sized churches 40% of transferring members came from this quarter. In the large churches just over 31%
came from this background – meaning that nearly 70% came
from churches without a Brethren link. Other surveys indicate
that this kind of transfer comes about because newcomers are
concerned about factors other than denominational loyalty
when choosing a church. This seems to bear that out.

Summary and Conclusions

The numbers of growing and declining churches are roughly in
balance, but it is the larger churches which are tending to grow,
while the smaller ones are in decline. There was an increase in
all categories of growth – biological growth, transfer and, most
hearteningly, conversion growth. The largest net rates of
increase came from the last source. Both larger and medium
churches have seen growth from conversions and churches,
both large and small have benefited from transfer growth. The

principal contributor to the net loss in the small churches was the death rate and this can be expected to continue as they have a high proportion – nearly 60% – of members over the age of 60. Unfortunately these small churches benefited less from biological growth since they have few young families. They were also seeing no conversion growth at all.

We have noted that small churches had broadly the same rate of transfer growth as the other two groups of churches. Two-thirds of this growth was fuelled by people moving to them from other Brethren churches. Also nearly one half of the growth came from people moving from other local churches in the local area. Though it is not possible to be certain from the data in the survey, the small churches (which, as can be seen from later chapters, were more traditional in their programmes and organisation) seem likely to have been the resort of people from small neighbouring Brethren churches which closed or who were disturbed by changes in the churches from which they came. This feature, together with the age profile and lack of conversion growth in the small churches, does not in general augur well for the continued life of small churches as a group. But, as can be seen from page 52, being a small church of Brethren background does not automatically condemn the church to ineffectiveness.

Larger churches are often accused of picking up transfer growth from other, often smaller, local churches. The survey did not find that they were more likely than others to source their growth in this way. Their transfer growth very often came from folk moving into the area from a distance, who more often than not did not come from a Brethren church. Clearly, in comparison with other local churches in the neighbourhood, their life, character (including non-denominational character?) and activities are attractive in an era of declining denominational loyalty among Evangelical Christians. These churches should, however, be concerned about a conversion growth rate of only about 1.5% a year, ie, for the normal larger church, about 1 or 2 persons a year. They need to be looking carefully at their evangelistic approaches, methods and attitudes, and the reasons for lack of impact. The ability to attract Christians moving into the area can mask poor performance in evangelism. In particular, in practice, 'seeker-friendly' programmes and style may be mainly 'incoming Christian friendly' programmes and style.

4

Activities and Services

Statistically, it is easier to ask churches what they do and how they organise than it is to ask what they are and what their style is. This chapter attempts to characterise the surveyed churches by their activities. Because of the nature of the earlier surveys, this approach permits some comparisons through time.

Each congregation was asked about their main activities and services. Over 70% of churches had a Breaking of Bread (or Communion) Service, a Prayer Meeting, a Bible Teaching activity, a Family Service and a Sunday School as Chart 20 indicates.

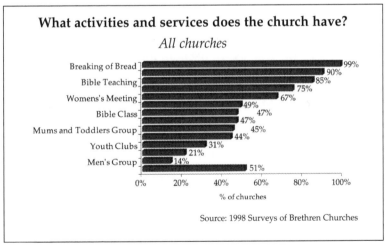

Chart 20: Activities and Services – All Churches

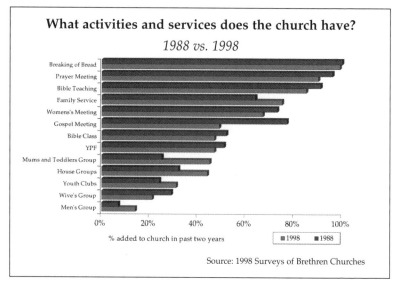

Chart 21: Activities and Services – All Churches – 1998 vs 1988

Chart 21 compares the activities and services with the 1988 situation. The most notable growth amongst principal activities was for Family Services. The number of churches holding them has risen to 75% from 64% – itself an increase from 43% back in 1978. However there has been a decline in incidence for a number of the other principal activities. Most notably the numbers holding a Gospel Meeting dropped to just under half from over three-quarters in 1988, which had already declined from 96% in 1978. Clearly the switch from Gospel Meetings to Family Services continues. There were also decreases for the following activities: Prayer meeting (-6%), Bible Teaching (-6%), Sunday School (-9%), Women's Meeting (-6).

Youth Activities also showed a slight decline with Bible Classes and YPF activities each falling below 50% for the first time, though Youth Clubs at 31% showed a growth of 7% on 1988. Mums and Toddlers Groups proved to be more popular, growing to 45% from 25% in 1988.

House Groups too were found in 44% of churches compared with 32% ten years earlier. Fourteen per cent of churches had a Men's Group compared with just 7% ten years ago, but Wives' Groups fell back to 21% from 29% in 1988.

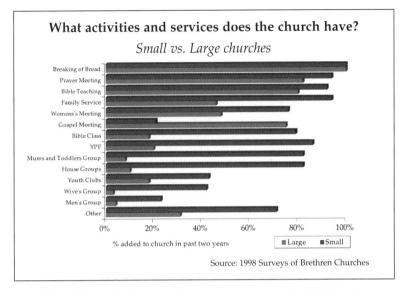

Chart 22: Activities and Services – Large vs Small Churches

Chart 22 shows the differing patterns of church life among large versus small churches. Large churches are much more likely to have a wide range of activities. Among large churches over 90% had the five principal activities mentioned earlier – Breaking of Bread (or Communion) Service, a Prayer Meeting, a Bible Teaching activity, a Family Service and a Sunday School. Well over three-quarters had a Women's Meeting, a Bible Class for teenagers, a YPF group, a Mums and Toddlers Group, and House Groups.

Small churches tended to concentrate their efforts. Over 80% had a Breaking of Bread service, a Prayer Meeting and a Bible Teaching activity, while 75% had a Gospel Meeting. This meeting continues at a high level in these churches – ten years previously 79% had a service like this, perhaps indicating a desire to keep to a traditional pattern of activities. Just under half of these churches had a Women's Meeting, and a Sunday School. Youth activities were present in only 20% of these churches, while Mums and Toddlers groups only figured in 8% of small churches. Obviously smaller churches do not have the resources to run a wide range of activities, but the absence of those aimed at families, particularly those with older children and teenagers, probably reflects the lifestage make-up of these churches with their principally elderly congregations. It does make growth more difficult for them, since many families with children transferring into an area will look for a church which can offer these kind of activities.

Teaching Services

Questions were asked about the teaching programme of the church. Chart 23 shows that 69% of churches claimed to have a Systematic Teaching Programme – exactly the same level as ten years ago. This was an increase though on 1978 when only one in two churches claimed to have one. Churches were asked which of their services and activities formed part of this programme.

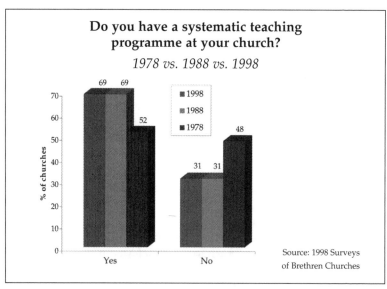

Chart 23: Systematic Teaching Programmes – 1998 vs 1988 vs 1978

Chart 24 shows the services which form part of the teaching programme. Most churches (85%) had a service which is intended to promote Bible teaching. In these churches – a high proportion, about 3 out of 4 – it formed part of the structured teaching programme. Some churches regarded their Family/Morning Service, where held, as part of the programme in 2 out of 3 cases. Where House Groups were held, these too were linked to the teaching programme in 5 out of 6 churches. The Breaking of Bread or Communion Service, almost universally held, had teaching on about half of the occasions. These services were by no means always tied into a structured programme of teaching

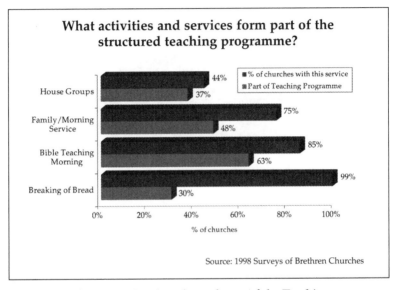

Chart 24 – Services deemed part of the Teaching Programme – All Churches

Churches were asked questions as to who spoke at these teaching services. Chart 25 shows that in 1998, 9 out of 10 churches used pre-arranged speakers at some time in the year for a teaching service, 85% used speakers from outside the church from time to time. In 2 out of 3 churches non-Brethren had been used as speakers in the past year, while 4 out of 10 churches used a full- or part-time worker for teaching. All these figures had increased on the situation 10 years previously, with the last two showing a substantial rise.

Chart 26 shows that at teaching meetings held by churches, the pattern is that normally the speaker is pre-arranged. The speaker is as likely to come from within the church as from outside. Less than 1 in 3 churches always used outside speakers.

Where there was a full- or part-time worker it was not usual for them to take all the teaching load. In 7 out of 10 churches they taught at less than half of the main teaching services.

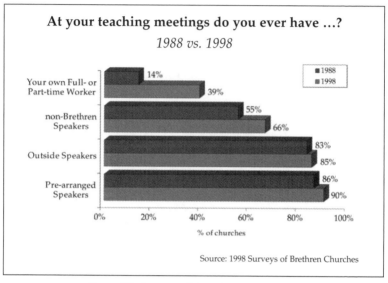

Chart 25: Source of Speakers at Services

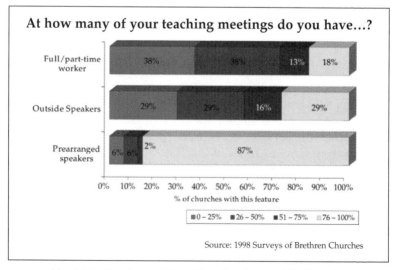

Chart 26: Speakers at Teaching Services – All Churches

Summary and Conclusions

The major change in the pattern of services is the continued rise in the popularity of Family Services, balanced by a decline in the number of churches holding Gospel Meetings. There is also a rise in the number of churches with House Groups, against a fall in the incidence of Prayer Meetings and midweek Bible Teaching meetings. The number of churches with Sunday Schools had declined as had those holding Women's Meetings. This pattern is probably as much a function of the age of those attending churches – fewer with families and fewer women available to run the Women's Meetings due to the increase in working women. It is none the less creditable to see that half of the small churches, though predominantly composed of the over 60s age group, are still concerned to continue with these outreaches.

There has been little spread of systematic teaching programmes against the position 10 years ago. The practice, formerly widespread, of having ministry after the Breaking of Bread service has gone for most churches. Teaching now takes place mainly in Morning/Family Services, Bible Teaching Meetings and House Groups.

The practice of full- or part-time workers being responsible for teaching in their churches is growing with their numbers in the churches, though they do not have, by any means, a monopoly of the teaching/preaching 'slots'. Indeed it is unusual for them to preach at as many as half of the main services.

Many churches continue to invite outside speakers to their services, but the number of churches using them has not changed, though there is a wider proportion of churches who are inviting speakers from non-Brethren backgrounds.

5

Worship and the Breaking of Bread

Worship

The 'Breaking of Bread' or Communion Service, in a distinctive form, has always played a central part in the lives of most Brethren churches. As we have seen, it is the most commonly held activity in these churches. Typically the service was held on Sunday morning at the 'prime time' for church members. Quite a number of churches however have adapted their Sunday morning programme to include a Family Service or a Morning Service more akin to the typical Sunday Service one might find in a Baptist or Methodist or, even, an Evangelical Anglican church. For many of these Brethren churches this has produced a tension as to which service should be given the time most convenient. Should the need to reach out to others – presumably the reason why the Family Service is being held – take precedence over the time traditionally assigned for communion? Some churches have tried to resolve the problem by incorporating communion within the Family Service, often at the expense of an open worship time, the traditional form of worship used by many Brethren churches.

Questions were therefore included in the survey to explore these issues. Churches were asked as to how they referred to their main worship service. Chart 27 shows their answers. Two out of three described it as a traditional Breaking of Bread service. Another 6% said that it was close to the traditional pattern. Twenty per cent described it variously as Morning Service (5%), Family Service (5%), All-age Worship (5%) or used another term.

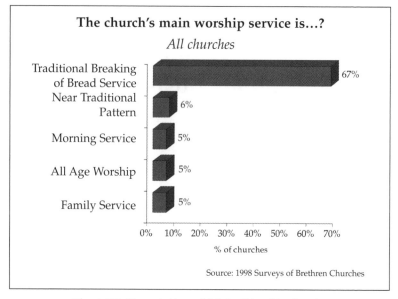

Chart 27: Description of Main Worship Service

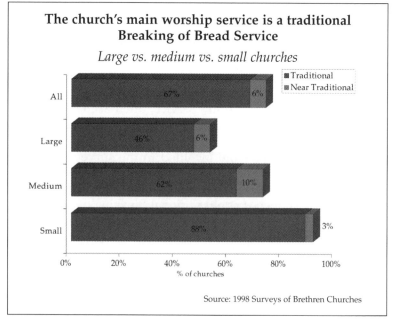

Chart 28: Breaking of Bread Service as Main Worship Service

Chart 28 shows the sort of Communion Service held by each church. Small churches were most likely to have a traditional Breaking of Bread Service (88%), followed by medium-sized churches (62%), while only 47% of large churches described their main worship as a Breaking of Bread Service. If those large churches with a 'nearly traditional' service are included, this only comes to just over 50% of this group.

The other kinds of service by type of church are shown in Chart 29.

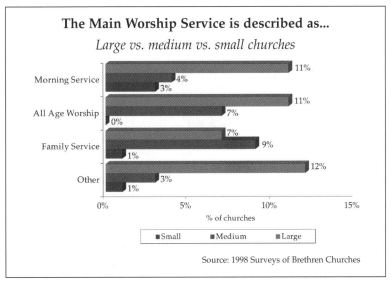

Chart 29: Other Services described as Main Worship Service

There is little in the way of a common thread in the composition of these services. Some described their service as being structured, with different elements of praise, worship, teaching, interviews etc. with sometimes communion being included. This led on to a further specific question about how the Communion/Breaking of Bread was observed.

Observing Communion

Chart 30 shows that for the overwhelming majority of churches Communion was always held in the church building (84%). In about half the churches (48%), it usually formed part of a service in which teaching was included. In a quarter of cases (23%) it was sometimes part of a Family Service, while in one in five churches (20%) it was observed in House Groups from time to time.

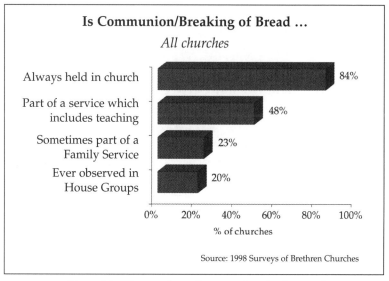

Chart 30: Places where Communion is observed

The patterns of observance between churches of different size is instructive. Chart 31 shows that small churches were most likely always to hold the Communion Service in the church building. They were also least likely to include it as part of a Family Service – only 8% of these churches did so while 50% of them have a Family Service from time to time. It is not surprising that only 8% of these small churches included it as part of a House Group, since only 10% have House Groups at all.

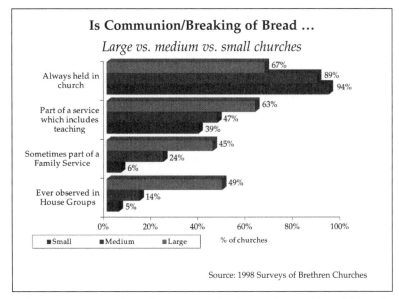

Chart 31: Places where Communion is observed – by Size of Church

Large-sized churches were most likely to break away from the traditions of the movement. Only two out of three always have communion in the church building. About half celebrate Communion in House Groups from time to time. Just under half of these large churches also sometimes have Communion as part of their Family (or Morning) Service. Two out of three include teaching in a service where Communion is held.

Medium-sized churches fall between the two groups with a tendency to be closer to the small church position.

Summary and Conclusions

Biblically, of course, worship is much wider than church services, let alone being typified by a single service such as the Breaking of Bread. It is the offering of all that we have and are to our Lord. Yet for many Brethren churches, this latter service has become synonymous with the term worship. The practice of breaking bread together with other Christians, in a simple ceremony, has been at the heart of the movement since its inception. Many of the facets of the service, such as open participation in

prayer, the use of devotional hymns focussing on the death of
Jesus Christ, the reading and exposition of scripture, are deeply
ingrained in the fabric of congregations. Brethren spirituality is
closely associated with celebration of the Lord's Supper in this
way and so any change in this area tends to be strongly resisted.
So much so that any move away from what are, in effect,
Brethren traditions handed down from past generations, is
regarded by some as almost a denial of the faith.

Thus churches which try to effect change in this area meet
considerable resistance. However it has to be said that this
resistance is often based more on emotional than biblical rea-
soning. It is clear that change in church life has to come. Churches must be able to adapt their programmes to the needs of
today's worshippers – particularly those with families. Many of
the larger churches have shown an ability to handle change in a
number of areas of church life, especially in this area of Communion, and so meet the needs of today's worshippers. Instead
of having worship services which are seen as irrelevant, unin-
volving, dull and sterile spiritually to young Christians, they are
seen as vibrant and motivating to faith and commitment, so that
evangelism is invigorated and enabled.

Many of the smaller churches in our sample, overwhelmingly populated by senior citizens, seemingly emphasising resistance to change in modes of worship, hymnbooks, and Bible ver-
sions, to name just a few of their practices, offer little that is
attractive to today's generation of young Christians and their
families. These people are looking for spiritual stimulus neces-
sary for nurturing faith, but these churches, bound up in observ-
ing practices which owe more to the past than to today's imper-
atives, seem unable and unwilling to walk the life of faith.
Hence these Christians turn away from churches which could
use their vigour and liveliness. They detect a spirituality which
has long since withdrawn into a ghetto, which is often no longer
able to deal with a 20th Century Church, let alone the bustling
world of the 21st Century which is crying out for a faith to com-
bat the essential emptiness of everyday life.

6

Evangelistic Methods

Evangelism continues to be an important focus of the activities of the surveyed churches. Though the methods used may change, it still has a priority in the programmes of most of these churches.

Each congregation was asked which evangelistic methods it uses or actively encourages. Chart 32 shows the principal forms mentioned. Top of the list is the Family Service. Nearly 3 out of 4 churches now feature these services. This is a major change from 1988 when just over 1 in 2 used them. The other change has been the decline in the Gospel Meeting. Back in 1978, 9 out of 10 churches had a regular Gospel Meeting, now only half that number do – just 43%. If anything the fall over the last 10 years has been faster, since 30% of churches dropped them in this period. Calendar events also featured in the programmes of more churches, with 7 out of 10 now having these – up +11% from 1988.

Just over half of all churches saw their package of youth activities as an evangelistic tool. This was described as a 'package of youth activities from cradle to adulthood'. This method had increased by +6% from the 1988 level. Emphasis on Friendship Evangelism was more marked – 56% of churches mentioning this as part of their outreach. This is a substantial gain on 10 years previously when just 33% mentioned it.

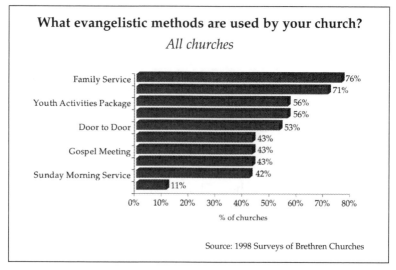

Chart 32: Evangelistic Methods used by Churches

Door to door activity was less used in 1998 – with 53% of churches utilising this method – down from 67% in 1988.

There has been a growth in popularity of Seekers' Bible Studies such as Alpha groups. 43% of churches had them in 1998. Ten years previously small group Bible studies were used evangelistically by only 23% of churches.

The Morning Service was also mentioned as a means of evangelism by 43% of churches. This ties up with the 43% of churches who run their Family Services each week on a Sunday morning.

Open Air Services – featured by 11% of churches – continue to decline in popularity. Back in 1978, 21% mentioned this form of witness.

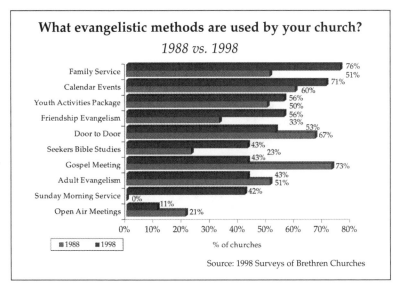

Chart 33: Evangelistic methods used – 1988 vs 1998

Large vs Small Churches

The patterns of evangelism in large and small churches differ markedly as shown in Chart 33. In large churches there is a wide range of activities. Nine out of ten of these churches run regular Family Services (92%), frequent Calendar Events and Guest Services (93%) and also have a Youth Activities Package (93%). Friendship Evangelism, Seekers' Bible Studies and adult evangelistic activities such as Men's Groups and Wives Meetings are all held by more than 2 out of 3 large churches.

On the other hand the most important evangelistic methods cited by small churches are Gospel Meetings (77%), Door to Door work (59%) and Open Air evangelism (16%) – all well above the incidence achieved amongst large churches. Family Services (51%) and Calendar Events (47%) feature in half the small churches.

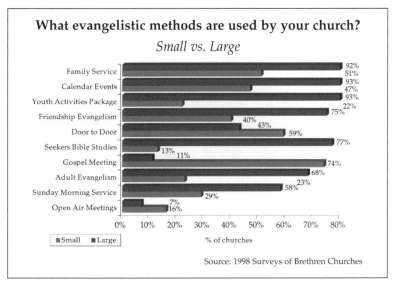

Chart 34: Evangelistic Methods – Large vs Small Churches

Chart 34 indicates that the change from the Gospel Meeting is most marked in large churches. In 1988, 64% of large churches had them in their programme. Ten years later this had fallen to just 11%. The level in small churches, by contrast, had declined by only 6% from 83% in 1988 to 77% in 1998.

Community Activities

A recognition of the lack of effectiveness to non-church goers of much of the evangelistic programme of the church has led many to focus on pre-evangelistic community activities. Chart 35 demonstrates the popularity of activities such as Parent and Toddler Clubs (47%) and Play Groups (11%) for families with younger children.

For children further up the age scale there are more activities geared to the children themselves. With the declining interest of many families in sending their children to Sunday School, many churches now run midweek Children's Clubs (58%). In addition to these or sometimes when there is not the manpower to run a regular activity, some churches run Holiday Clubs (52%), aimed at children during the school holidays with a burst of activity over a week or so.

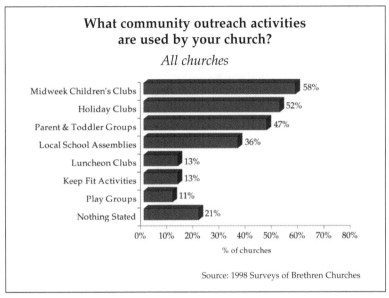

What community outreach activities are used by your church?

All churches

Chart data:
- Midweek Children's Clubs: 58%
- Holiday Clubs: 52%
- Parent & Toddler Groups: 47%
- Local School Assemblies: 36%
- Luncheon Clubs: 13%
- Keep Fit Activities: 13%
- Play Groups: 11%
- Nothing Stated: 21%

% of churches

Source: 1998 Surveys of Brethren Churches

Chart 35: Community Outreach Activities – All Churches

Some churches concentrate on the needs of the elderly, with luncheon clubs (13%), specifically to reach out to this group (though the proportion is perhaps surprisingly low, considering the high proportion of churches with a large elderly membership).

Keep Fit Groups (13%) also target others such as women in particular. For many of these groups there is little specifically 'religious' or evangelistic content. Rather they are seen as a method of contacting people in the local area, serving the needs found in the community, and offering an opportunity for friendship and pre-evangelistic contact. These activities are much more likely to be found in the larger churches as Chart 36 shows.

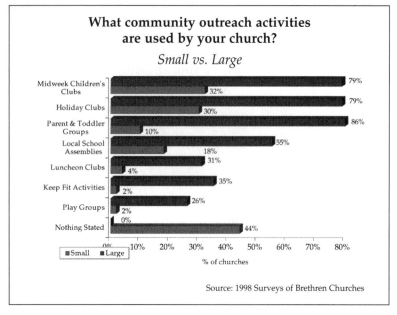

Chart 36: Community Outreach Activities – Large vs Small Churches

Summary and Conclusions

Evangelistic activities have a high priority in the programmes of these churches, both for young people and old. They are the third leg of the tripod on which the church builds. Despite emphasis on this activity, its effectiveness in bringing about conversions has not been great in the past and many churches have devoted time, thought and effort to what changes might be made. Many larger churches have tried changing the pattern and content of their major services to attract and hold families, through family-friendly services, but have also tried to make their programmes attractive through all-age youth packages. Smaller churches often lack the manpower to follow the latter course, but they also seem to lack the willingness to change from traditional methods such as Gospel Meetings, even though there has been little in the way of conversions over many years.

Most evangelistic methods rely on folk coming in to activities

and services. Data from elsewhere shows fewer people attending church on a regular basis, particularly the unchurched. During the past twenty years the English Churches Attendance survey has shown that the church has lost large numbers of children and teenagers attending Sunday Schools and Bible Classes.
It seems likely from this survey that this is also true of Brethren
churches too. If these activities which have been a prime method
of recruitment in the past into the body of the church, and prime
evangelistic –type services are also failing, it is hard to see how
many churches can survive for very much longer. The relevance
and effectiveness of evangelistic activities must be a matter of
prime concern for churches and their leaderships. The results of
evangelism in these churches is the subject of the next chapter.

7

Conversions and Baptisms

For years Gospel Meetings – services with a focus on evangelistic preaching – were one of the principal services of Brethren churches. Though there has been a move away from calling the event by this name, a concern to convey the Good News is never far from the heart of these churches. Many other of the activities are also concerned with reaching out to various groups of people, young and old, with evangelism as a principal aim. The survey sought to discover how effective the churches are, not just at reaching people but also making disciples. This would include the process of bringing them to faith in Christ and then helping build them into the church as they respond in baptism.

The survey questioned respondents about numbers who had been converted during the previous two years as well as the numbers who had been baptised. Collecting accurate data in this area is not easy. It is relatively simple for most churches to be clear about the number of people who have been baptised in a two-year period – always providing records are accurately kept. However estimating the numbers of conversions is a more hazardous exercise. The journey to faith is different for each person and it is often difficult to know whether or not there has been a clear commitment to Christ in the absence of the sort of public declaration often accompanying baptism or 'making a decision' at an evangelistic rally. While the movement has historically placed strong emphasis on knowing when any 'decision for Christ' has been made, observation suggests that there is a greater readiness these days to accept that this commitment may consciously only be known by a person in retrospect. For reasons like these, leaders of churches may be less ready to answer a question on numbers of conversions. Indeed, some observed that ' the Lord knows the hearts of men', indicating that they may not know their flock quite that well. We should not be surprised, then, if at least a quarter of churches declined to answer this question, compared with only 4% who did not complete the questions on the size of the church.

Number of Conversions

Chart 37 below shows the number of people who were thought to have come to faith – with the non-respondents included in the percentages.

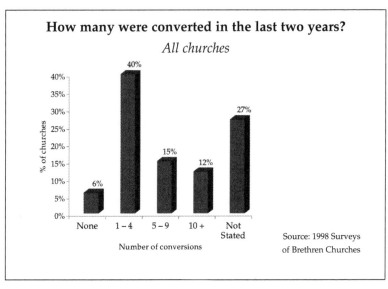

Chart 37: Number of Conversions reported by All Churches

In only 6% of the churches, who did reply to the question, were there no claimed conversions in the past two years. Forty per cent estimated that between 1 and 4 people had been converted in this period, 15% between 5 and 9 and in 12% of churches the number was 10 or more. The figures are not strictly comparable with previous years, when the numbers not replying were included in the 'no conversion' figure. In 1988, 29% of churches were estimated to have had no conversions. Looking deeper, it seems that 4% of the churches refusing to reply to this question had estimated that some adult converts had joined the church. If one subtracts this number from the non-responses and adds in the 6% of churches with no conversions, the figure of 29% is arrived at – the same level as 1988. This may indicate that the levels are comparable. It could also suggest that non-response to the question is another way of saying 'no conversions'. At the top of the range of response, the figure of 12% reporting 10 or more conversions in 1998 is way below the figure of 19% of churches in 1988, and 20% in 1978.

Conversions by Size of Church

It is of interest to look at the answers by size of church. We might expect large churches to have more conversions, as the figures in Chart 38 bear out.

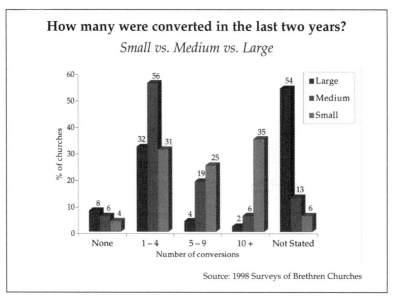

Chart 38: Conversion reported – by Size of Church

Thirty-five per cent of the large churches had had 10 or more conversions in the previous two years – 13 churches reporting over 20. Twenty-five per cent had had between 5 and 9, and a further 31% between 1 and 4 conversions in the period. Only 4% reported no conversions and 6% of these large churches declined to reply to this question. It was in the small churches

where a large proportion also declined to answer the question –
over 54% making no reply. A further 8% reported no conversions in the period, while 6% of these small churches reported 5
or more. Small church size is no barrier to conversions, though,
since one small church had 20 in this period of whom 14 were
adults. Medium-sized churches fell between the two extremes.

Adults vs Children

Chart 39 below indicates the number of adults or children converted in the study period.

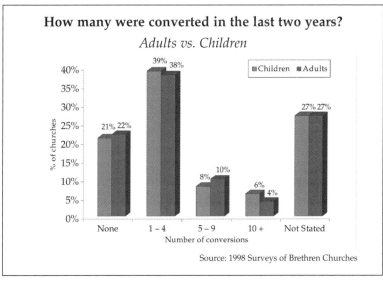

Chart 39: Conversion reported – Adults vs Children

The most obvious finding is that, adding together 'None'
with 'Not stated', just under half (48%) had no adult conversions and 49% no conversions of children. The split between
adults and children is fairly even, across the range of replies –
though not necessarily at the level of the individual church.
Only 4% of churches reported 10+ conversions of children, less
than the 6% of churches reporting 10+ conversions of adults. In
previous surveys it was usual to see more conversions of children than adults being reported, so a significant change may be

in process here.

Change in Adult Conversions against Previous Years

There has been a rise in the numbers of churches recording no adult conversions, but there is good news in the number of churches claiming 5 or more.

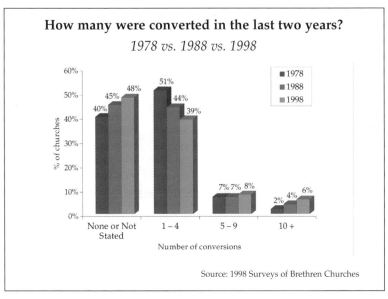

How many were converted in the last two years?
1978 vs. 1988 vs. 1998

Source: 1998 Surveys of Brethren Churches

Chart 40: Adults converted in Previous Two Years – 1978 vs 1988 vs 1998

Chart 40 shows that over the twenty-year period the number of churches reporting no adult conversions has increased from 40% to 48%. The number of churches reporting between 1 and 4 adults being converted dropped back from 51% to 39%. At the higher end of the range there is a heartening growth of the % of churches reporting 10 or more adults being converted. Six per cent of churches had 10+ adult conversions compared with 4% back in 1988, and 2% in 1978. This is not entirely unexpected since the growth of the larger churches has already been noted and many of these are experiencing considerable growth through adult conversions.

Numbers of Baptisms

Baptism in these churches follows on from conversion, though not necessarily straight after, especially in the case of children of a young age. There is fairly close correspondence between the numbers reported on conversions and for baptisms. Chart 41 below shows the numbers of churches reporting baptisms.

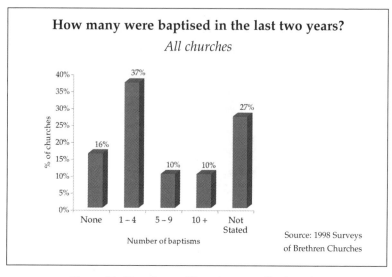

Chart 41: Numbers of Baptisms – All Churches

57% of churches reported at least one baptism during the two-year period – but whereas only 6% of churches recorded 'no conversions', 16% reported 'no baptisms'. 10% of churches had 10 baptisms or more, a further 10% between 5 and 9 and a third of churches (37%) between 1 and 4.

Adults vs Children

Chart 42, shown next, compares the % of churches reporting baptisms of children as against adults.

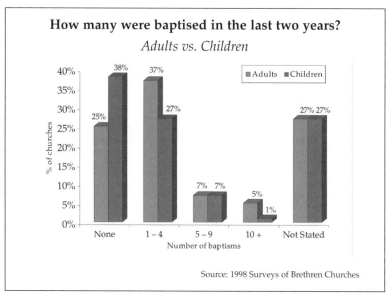

Chart 42: Baptisms – Adults vs Children – All Churches

The lower numbers of churches reporting baptisms as against conversions might indicate that churches are less likely to baptise a child before the teenage years while still accepting the reality of the child's conversion.

While 48% of churches reported baptising at least one adult, only 35% recorded baptism of a child, and while 4% reported conversions of 10 or more children, only 1% recorded baptising that number.

The figures for adults are much closer together. For instance 6% of churches reported 10 or more conversions, while 5% reported baptising that number.

Baptisms by Size of Church

As expected, the large churches report most baptisms and small churches are likely to have few if any.

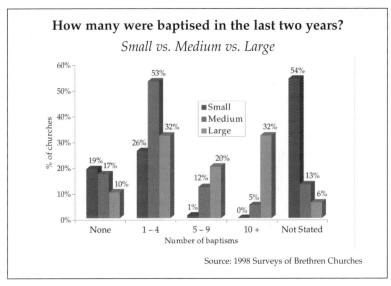

Chart 43: Baptisms – by Size of Church

Chart 43 shows that 82% of large churches reported baptisms, 70% of medium-sized, but only 27% of small churches. Most medium-sized churches reported between 1 and 4 baptisms with only 1% recording more than this number. Just under a third of large churches had between 1 and 4 baptisms, a further 20% had between 5 and 9, while 32% – a third – had baptised 10 or more people. 6 churches had baptised over 20 people.

Looking at the overall numbers of baptisms by church size, large churches with 45% of attendances recorded 50% of baptisms, medium churches with 38% of the church attendances reported 35% of baptisms and the small churches with 17% of attendance accounted for 15% of baptisms.

This suggests that it may be the medium churches who are not getting quite their 'fair share' of baptisms, while larger churches were more likely to have a larger share. But small does not have to mean ineffective in this area. Ten of the small churches accounted for half the baptisms in this group – an average of 6 a church. Although they only had 2% of attendances they accounted for 6% of all baptisms recorded and 7% of conversions.

Summary and Comment

This is a sensitive area and data is incomplete, but it does seem as if the number of churches reporting no baptisms or no conversions is rising. Just under 1 in 3 churches do not report conversions and just under 1 in 2 no baptisms.

Small churches are least likely to report conversions or baptisms. This may not be unexpected when given their elderly age profile with 70% of the congregations over 60 years old.

However, growth through conversion is an important contributor to the overall growth of the movement, as we saw in an earlier chapter.

Small churches can be vigorous and effective in witness and discipling as shown by the 10 small churches with an average of 6 conversions each. Those 38% of small churches which reported conversions actually had as many conversions as the 14 churches with over 200 members each, despite only having half the level of congregation attending overall.

This does not mean that larger churches were lagging. They account for almost half of all conversions. This is slightly more than their 'fair' share of both baptisms and conversions – i.e. greater than attendance share. But the size is not a guarantee of vigour or effectiveness. 40% of this group reported less than 4 conversion in a two-year period.

8

Leadership

Each congregation was asked about the form of leadership arrangements that they had. The results are shown in Chart 44.

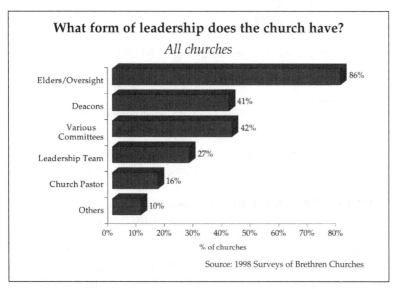

Chart 44: Form of Church Leadership – 1998

Practically all churches claimed to have at least some kind of formal leadership. 86% referred to it as a group of Elders or the Oversight. Fewer churches had an oversight/elders group than in 1988 – down by 6% from the '88 level of 92%, which had itself been maintained at the 1978 level.

One in 10 churches – mostly smaller – had a Brothers Meeting as their form of leadership. This figure has shown a slight increase from the '88 level, perhaps because of the greater number of small churches about.

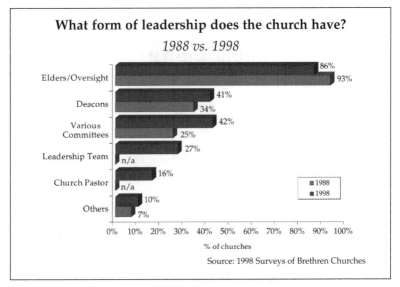

Chart 45: Form of Leadership – 1998 vs 1988

For the first time in these surveys, Leadership Teams are mentioned. 27% of churches responding had one of these. We can deduce from these figures that in about half the churches with a team like this it must run alongside or overlap with the elders/oversight. In addition 16% of churches referred to the Church Pastor as part of the leadership of the church. We did not formally ask in previous surveys how many pastors and full-time workers were involved in the leadership of the church, so it is not possible to say whether this is an increase or not. Since 33% of churches claimed to have a full- or part-time worker, it would indicate that for about half this number this worker was a full member of the leadership group of the church but for about half of these cases the worker was not regarded as such. We did not ask follow-up questions on this point but anecdotal evidence indicates that the failure to involve paid workers fully in the leadership of the church is a continuing source of friction.

Subsidiary Leadership Groups

41% of churches had a group of Deacons in 1998 – an increase of 7% on the 1988 level. Other committees are also mentioned by 42% of churches, which was a very big increase from the 1988 level when 13% of churches claimed to have these involved in leadership. Here, there is a significant development in the administration of churches of Brethren background.

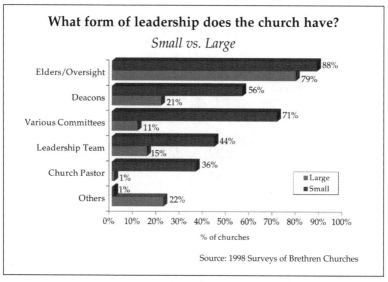

What form of leadership does the church have?

Small vs. Large

Elders/Oversight	88% / 79%
Deacons	56% / 21%
Various Committees	71% / 11%
Leadership Team	44% / 15%
Church Pastor	36% / 1%
Others	1% / 22%

Legend: Large, Small

% of churches

Source: 1998 Surveys of Brethren Churches

Chart 46: Form of Leadership – Large vs Small Churches

The difference in the various forms of leadership between churches of differing sizes is shown in Chart 46.

It indicates that 44% of the large churches have a leadership team and 88% of them an elders/oversight group, showing a high degree of overlap. While 36% of large churches had a designated Pastor, only 1% of smaller churches had one. These smaller churches were much less likely to have extra committees too. Eighteen per cent had Deacons and only 9% various other committees. In the larger churches, possibly because of the much wider range of activities groups and responsibilities, 56% had a group of Deacons and 71% had other various committees.

Leadership Meetings

Chart 47 shows the frequency of meetings of the Leadership Group.

In 8% of churches the main Leadership meets weekly. This is close to the level observed in 1988. In 1 in 5 churches the group meets fortnightly – a higher level than ten years before. Mostly the group meets monthly or less often.

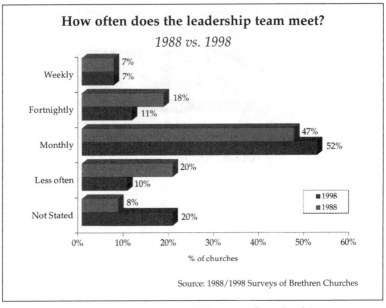

Chart 47: Frequency of Meeting of Leadership

The main Leadership group in larger churches, were no more likely to meet weekly than in other churches. However 40% had a meeting once a fortnight. In only 2% of small churches was there anything like this frequency.

The leaderships of small churches showed a reluctance to meet formally like this. 27% meet monthly while 45% do so less frequently than that and 17% omitted to state a frequency.

One in four leadership groups meet for special retreats or weekends. This is up from 19% in 1988. Larger churches are much more likely to do so as they are held by groups in 2 out of 3 of these churches.

Appointment of Leaders

Generally the church leaders are chosen by the current group of leaders alone. Chart 47 shows that forty-five per cent of churches in 1998 used this method. This is down from 66% in 1988. In another 38% of churches' leaders were chosen by the current leadership group in consultation with the church – a rise of 7% from 1988. Leaders were elected in 7% of churches.

Women in Leadership

The increasing extent to which women are in positions of responsibility, already noted in 1988, has continued. In this survey only 1% of churches had women as elders – the same as in 1998. However women were included in the Leadership Teams of 21% of churches. This suggests that they are present on 3 out of 4 of the Leadership Teams in churches with this form of leadership. Over 1 in 5 churches had women Deacons. As 2 in 5 churches had Deacons, women are present in this group in half the relevant churches.

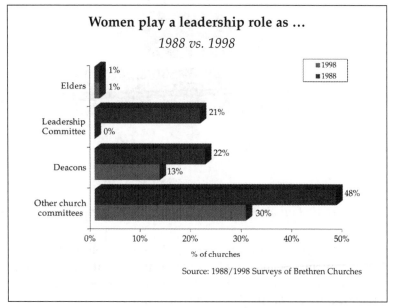

Chart 48: Women in Leadership – 1998 vs 1988

Women were also much more likely to be present on other church committees – appearing in committees in practically every church with this form of organisation.

Paid Workers

Chart 49 shows the number of churches with a full- or part-time paid worker. One in three of the churches had workers whose ministry was part of the life of the church, i.e. they were not a full-time Christian worker who was based in the church but worked elsewhere.

This compares with a level of 1 in 5 ten years previously – a substantial increase, itself double the level of 1 in 10 churches back in 1978.

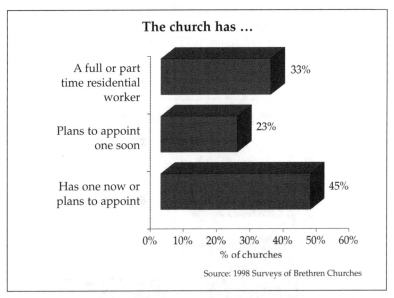

Chart 49: Full- or Part-Time Resident Workers in Churches

These resident workers were much more likely to be in the larger churches. Seven out of ten of the larger churches had someone in this category in 1998, over twice as many as ten years previously. Only 9% of small churches had someone employed either full- or part-time. While this was well above the position in 1988, they are still no doubt inhibited by the costs of employment.

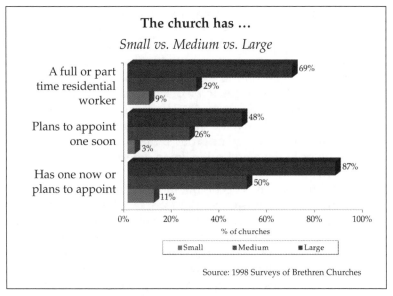

Chart 50: Plans for appointing Resident Workers in Churches

These levels look set to increase still further in the future, since 45% of churches reported that they would have a worker in place or had plans to employ one in the next two years.

Objectives

Vision statements and written objectives are increasingly popular in the world of business and secular organisations. They are increasingly used too in churches. Forty-five per cent of churches have either a vision statement or a set of written objectives, 1 in 3 churches has a vision statement – double the number in 1988, 1 in 4 churches has a statement of written objectives.

Large churches were four times more likely to have either of these than small churches.

Summary and Conclusions

The patterns of leadership in the churches are changing – faster in the larger churches than elsewhere. While practically all churches have a structured leadership of some sort, larger churches have much more complex structures. This reflects the range of activities but also the need for greater flexibility in these structures. Change is demanding of leadership time and, with the increasing rapidity of development, many churches have found it is becoming ever more difficult to find enough time to cover all that needs to be decided and organised within the normal leadership groups. They are also finding that devolving responsibility for much of the operation of church activities to a wide range of groups, many of them containing women, helps to develop leadership in others, and enables them to use their gifts.

At the same time it is becoming more difficult for lay leaders, busy with the demands of secular jobs, families etc. to find the time to devote to church activities. One way around meeting the increasing demands of running a church and overseeing the regular routine is to recruit paid full- and part-time workers to help with the task. This has worked well in some cases. In most of the very large churches there is a core of 'professional' leadership which has no doubt enabled the church to grow.

Women in the church

We have already seen that women play a more important role in the organisational structures of these churches than ten years before. Their role in the leadership of the churches has expanded in this period. Nearly 2 out of 3 churches said that they had a role of some sort on a committee, though for very few was it in the upper reaches of leadership in the church.

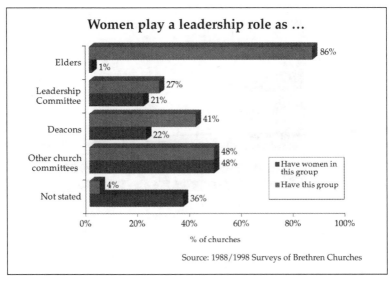

Chart 51: Women in Leadership – 1998

From Chart 51 it can be seen that only 1% of churches had women as Elders, while 86% had a committee of Elders or an Oversight group. Twenty-seven per cent of churches had a Leadership Team, but women were included in this group in only 21% of churches. Forty-one per cent of churches had a group of Deacons, but women were included in this group in only about half of cases. For churches with other committees there seem to be a general acceptance that women could be included in these committees (though this might be because the committees cover areas historically thought of as 'women's areas' – such as the Women's Meeting or Sunday School activities).

Large Vs Small Churches

The position varies widely by church size. Chart 52 shows that the larger churches make more use of women in their structures. Only 7% of these churches did not have women playing a part in committees of one sort or another. In small churches it seems that women do not play a formal role in over 70% of cases.

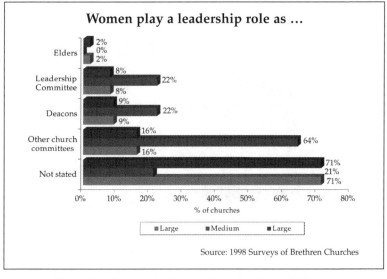

Chart 52: Women in Leadership – by Size of Church

Forty per cent of the large churches had women as part of a Leadership Committee but in only 2% were they known as Elders. Thirty-nine per cent of large churches had women as Deacons and in 74% they played a part in other committees.

In only 2% of small churches were women designated as Elders and in 8% they formed part of the Leadership Team – half of those churches with a group like this. In small churches only 21% had a groups of Deacons, and 9% of these churches allow women to serve in this way. The small churches had few other committees, so it is not surprising that not many have women serving on them.

Involvement in Church Services

Historically the active involvement of women in church services has not been encouraged in these churches. Data from a previous survey in 1978 is not strictly comparable, so that direct comparisons cannot be made as to trends. Chart 53 below shows the extent to which women were permitted in 1998-89 to take part audibly in main church services.

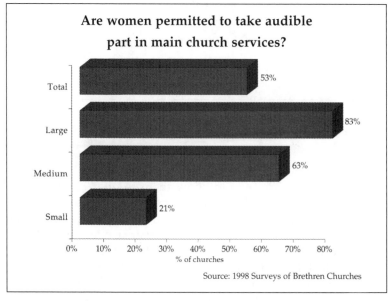

Chart 53: Women's Participation in Services

In just over half of churches women are permitted to take audible part. In the large churches this level rises to 83%, but in the small churches only 21% allow women to participate audibly.

Form of Participation

Churches were questioned about what forms of verbal participation were permitted. Chart 53 shows that a few of the churches who had said they would not allow women to participate verbally, nonetheless allowed a very limited range of participation, so some of the following figures are higher than the overall data.

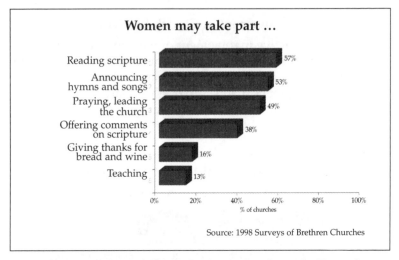

Chart 53: Women's Participation in Services – by Type of Contribution

57% said they would permit women to read aloud from scripture, while only 38% would allow them to offer comments on what had been read. In 53% women were able to announce hymns and songs, while just under half (49%) permitted women to lead the church in prayer. Two other areas were included in this part of the survey, but participation was at a much lower level. In just 16% of churches women were permitted to give thanks for the bread and wine in the Communion (or Breaking of Bread) Service. Lower still was the number of churches which permitted women to teach (or expound) scripture. In only 13% of churches were women allowed to do this in main church services.

In 1978 churches were asked if women should be allowed to pray audibly in the prayer meeting (specifically). Thirty-six per cent said that they ought to be able to do so. The levels in 1998 are thus some 20% higher. A question was also asked 20 years ago whether women should be allowed to speak 'at the Breaking of Bread meeting'. Only 20% of churches thought they should. There appears to have been a much bigger shift in the number of churches permitting such a practice, since the current levels for this could be about 35% higher.

As might be expected, the levels of women's participation vary markedly by size of church. Chart 55 indicates that in large churches over 3 out of 4 allowed women to read scripture, pray or announce hymns or songs, while 2 out of 3 also permitted them to offer comments on scripture. Medium-sized churches were at a slightly lower level for these activities. In small churches only 1 in 4 allowed participation by women in these ways.

Women were allowed to give thanks for the bread and wine in 38% of the large churches and to expound scripture in 27% of them. The level of these activities was much lower in medium-sized churches and almost non-existent in the small churches.

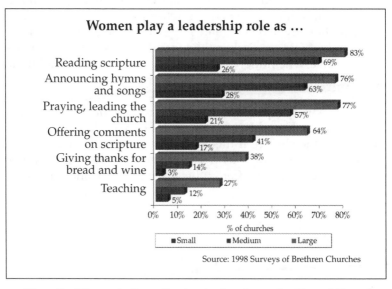

Chart 54: Women's Contribution in Services – by Size of Church

Summary and Conclusions

The level of participation of women in church life has changed
considerably over the past years. This is true in church services
and in the day-to-day running of the church. In the Breaking of
Bread Service twenty years ago only 1 in 5 churches permitted
women to participate audibly. Now this kind of participation by
women probably occurs in more than 50% of churches. Women
are also playing a bigger part in church structures and leadership, particularly in the everyday running of committees etc.
While some churches permit them to serve with church Leadership Teams, there would appear to be some way to go before
they are fully accepted as the equal of men in these roles. It must
be pointed out, too, that while we have been discussing whether
women's participation takes place in churches at all, it is not the
same as the amount of activity accounted for by women within
a church, as compared with that by men. Anecdotal evidence
indicates that churches have a long way to go before women
play a part commensurate with either their numbers or gifting.

It might be expected that as churches contract in size, there
would be increased pressure to allow women to participate.
Thus one might expect small churches to have higher levels of
participation by women than larger churches. This does not
seem to be the case. Perhaps the fact that these small churches
have an overwhelmingly older profile means that the ability to
change is inhibited by the principles, habits and practices of a
lifetime.

It is also worth speculating that one reason for churches moving ahead and growing is due to their releasing the gifts of
women in the church. If this is so then there may well be room
for much more growth as it is realised that there is so much
more that women can offer in the worship, work and witness of
the church.

10

Missionary Activity

Missionary activities and interest – particularly in cross-cultural mission – have played a significant part in the life of Brethren Churches from the earliest days. The indications are that for most churches of this background this is still the case. Chart 56 shows that, in 1988, 75% of churches indicated that they had regular missionary activities and ten years later in 1998 this figure had risen to 77%.

As might be expected this level of interest is higher in the larger and medium-sized churches with a range of activities being represented in their church life as Chart 57 bears out. However it is worth noting that, for many smaller churches as well, this was also part of their regular church life. In 1998, 90% of the larger churches had regular missionary activities, compared with 85% of medium-sized while 62% of the smaller churches also concentrated on missionary matters, despite, as we shall see, the relatively low level of missionaries actually commended from churches of small size.

Variety of Missionary Activities

Churches were asked in 1998 what form the 'missionary activities' took. Chart 58 shows that 64% provided missionary topics in regular services while 43% had missionary meetings for the whole church. Over half had prayer meetings focusing on missionary topics. Thirty-three per cent went as far as having a special Missionary Day to concentrate on this aspect of church life. Just under one in five churches had a missionary 'Sewing Meeting' – historically these have concentrated, as the name suggests, on making and providing garments and items for missionary-related activities in various countries. They have been almost always run by the women of the church and they have

combined this practical help with stimulating missionary interest in individual missionaries and in prayer for them. Missionary study classes which were a feature of the life of many
churches in the earlier part of the century appear to have more
or less died out. Only 2% of churches have these now.

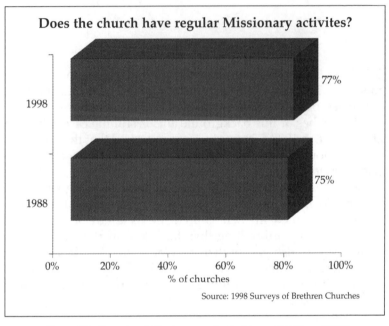

Chart 56: Regular Missionary Activities – 1998 vs 1988

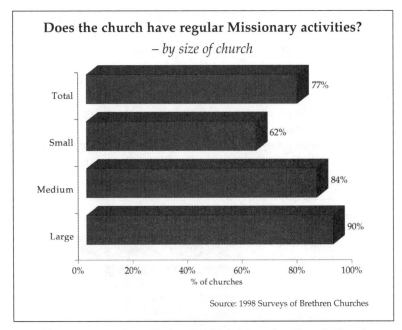

Chart 57: Regular Missionary Activities – by Size of Church

The situation by size of church, shown in Chart 59, indicates that, as might be expected, the medium and larger churches have a wider range of activities than is possible in the smaller churches. They have the ability to run more activities and to concentrate resource in this area.

Large churches were more likely to include items of missionary interest and activity in their regular services – with 85% of them following this practice. Seventy per cent of the medium-sized churches did this, compared with only 45% of the smaller churches. This may reflect the type of services held in the different size of churches. No doubt many in the smaller churches would think that these items were not suitable for inclusion in a Communion Service or some of the other activities which predominate there.

The proportion of churches holding regular missionary prayer meetings ranged between 43% and 58% depending on the size of the church. Data on the frequency of these was not requested. As we have seen, churches showed their interest in promoting news of missionary interest by holding meetings designed to appeal to the whole church. About half the medium- and large-sized churches did this and about 30% of the small churches.

Special missionary days were featured in half of the larger churches, about a third of the medium churches and just under a fifth of the small churches. The presence or absence of a link with a commended missionary only added a little to the evidence of 'missionary-mindedness' as evidenced by a slightly higher level of these activities in the life of the church.

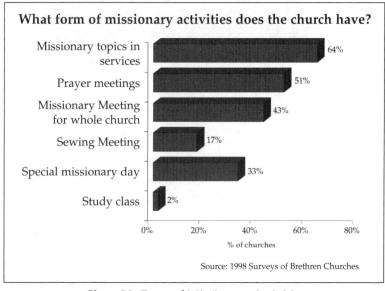

Chart 58: Form of Missionary Activities

Missionary Activity 77

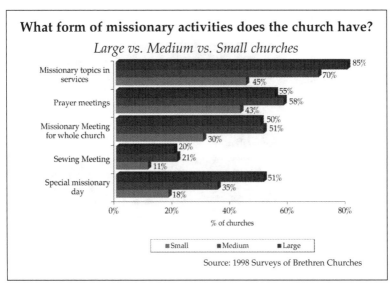

Chart 59: Form of Missionary Activities – by Size of Church

Commendation of Missionaries

Chart 60 indicates that nearly half of all churches (44%) had people whom they had commended to missionary service. This is the same level as was found ten years previously. The majority of this 44% are people who have been called to a long-term commitment – 39% of churches had someone with whom they had this kind of relationship. In recent years people have also been involved in short-term service commitments often via agencies such as Operation Mobilisation and Gospel Literature Overseas. Fourteen per cent of churches had commended people to these short-term stints in missionary work. Chart 61, which shows the data by size of church, shows that the larger churches are almost five times as likely to have commended short- or long-term missionaries as small churches – much the same as ten years previously. Given the average size (and age-profile) of these churches compared with the group we have labelled 'small', it is hardly surprising if the latter do not have recent missionaries sent out from their church. Medium-sized churches come midway between the two on commendation.

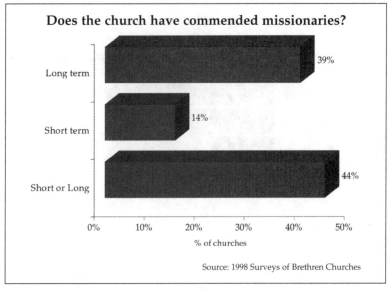

Chart 60: Missionaries commended from the church

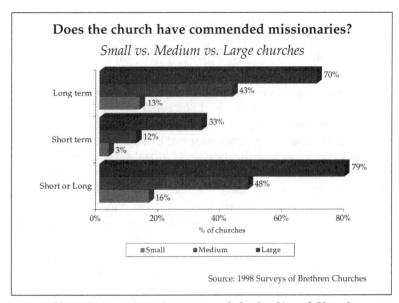

Chart 61: Missionaries commended – by Size of Church

Summary and Conclusions

Missionary activities seem to play as important a part in the life of these churches as ten years before. Some have noted a decline in interest in missionary activity as shown by the demise of the large national missionary rallies, which were a feature of the early post-war period. As many churches claim to have commended missionaries as in 1988. Thus interest in mission as determined by what churches are doing – as compared with what we might think the level of interest is – continues to hold up. It is true that there is not the same level of interest in national missionary conferences and suchlike, but churches obviously hold it as an important part of their church life. It is good to see, too, that larger churches are leading the way in stimulating interest in the topic, since anecdotal evidence suggests that they are often thought to have little interest beyond their own boundaries.

11

Charismatic Phenomena and Practice

The Charismatic movement since 1960 has presented chal-
lenges for all Christian groupings, particularly those of long-
standing Evangelical commitment. Some congregations have
been influenced to such an extent that it would now be appro-
priate to describe them as Charismatic. Quite apart from
acceptance of the label, other congregations have been influenced in doctrine on certain practices and phenomena, in the
character of their activities (particular in worship style, music
and hymnody), and in the freedom given for the use of Charismatic gifts. They have done so without becoming Charismatic
churches. (It is interesting that recent work by Christian
Research suggests that over the last decade a proportion of
churches describing themselves as Charismatic at the end of the
1980s are now inclined to describe themselves as 'mainstream
Evangelical'. This may imply that Charismatic practice is now
such an accepted part of mainstream Evangelicalism that those
formerly describing themselves as Charismatic no longer feel
the need to distinguish themselves in this way.)

The probability is that churches included in this survey fall
mainly into the second of the two groups just described. Some
have indeed actively sought to bridge the gap between Charismatic and 'mainstream' Evangelical churches, eg, by allowing or
even encouraging the exercise of Charismatic gifts, while not
regarding it, formally or informally, as mandatory either in indi-
viduals or the standard practice of the congregation. Some of the
congregations are known to have sought to include both those
with Charismatic experience and those without it – though they
have not always in the long run avoided open or unspoken dis-
sension on the issues.

The 1998-99 survey did not ask questions which bear on doctrinal positions on the matter, or on worship style, music, etc. As in 1988, questions were asked about practice of Charismatic gifts in the congregation.

Inclusion of Tongues, Prophecy and Healing in Services

Churches were asked if in any of the services of the church tongues are used, prophecy given or healing take place. Chart 62 shows the occurrence of each of these.

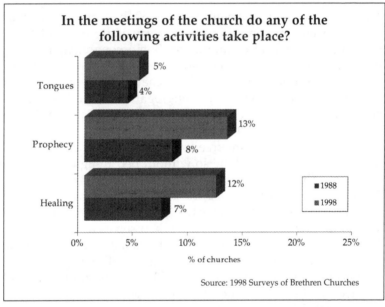

Chart 62: Occurrence of Tongues, Prophecy, Healing

Tongues are used publicly in only 5% of churches – a slight increase on the position ten years previously. Prophecies are given from time to time in 13% of churches – which is well up on the position in 1988. The practice is found or used in only a limited minority of churches. Healing takes place in services in 12% of churches – up from 7% ten years before.

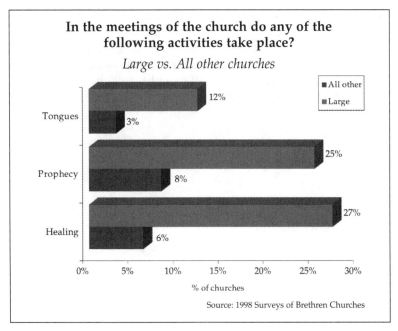

Chart 63: Occurrence of Tongues, etc. – by Size of Church

It is clear from Chart 63 that large churches are far more likely to allow these activities in the public meetings of the church.

One in four of the large churches practice healing gifts in public services and about the same percentage allow prophecies to be given. The public use of tongues seems to be less widespread in these churches. In all other churches, the incidence of any of these activities is fairly rare.

Summary and Conclusions

The Charismatic movement, as evidenced by the use of tongues, prophecies and gifts of healing, has not made great inroads into Brethren churches. Even in the larger churches, these practices are scarcely part of the stuff of everyday church life. No doubt the advocates of a more open approach to this view of spirituality will argue that these are the growing churches. It is worth noting that growth seems to come to all kinds of church and that the use or otherwise of these charismatic gifts is only one aspect of what causes churches to move ahead. The Spirit seems to laugh at our easy explanations for guaranteed church growth.

Though the percentages are still low, the extent of change in the 1990s was significant. Questions about doctrinal position on these issues, and about style might well have suggested more extensive penetration, at least in the large- and medium-sized churches.

12

Interdenominational Links

Historically, Open Brethren churches in the UK, and particularly in England, have tended to oscillate between an open-hearted, non-denominational view of the church, and a sectarian view in which Brethren churches have kept themselves to themselves and, even, have gone to the extent of regarding themselves as the only right ecclesiastical form. This chapter explores practice on interdenominational matters so as to illuminate current attitudes on this broad question.

Links with other Churches

Churches were questioned about any links they might have with other churches and organisations. The list included membership of the Evangelical Alliance, and links with a local Council of Churches or the 'Churches Together' group in their locality. They were also asked about whether they had links with other Brethren churches, other local Evangelical churches or a 'twinning arrangement' with a church overseas.

Most churches (85%) have some links with other Brethren churches – at the same level as ten years previously. Nearly as many have contacts with other local evangelical churches (78%). This figure shows a considerable increase on the 1988 level of 59%. So too does the membership of the Evangelical Alliance which has also doubled from a level of 18% in 1988 to 38% in 1998.

Churches were also asked about their links with other local churches via organisations such as the local Council of Churches or 'Churches Together' in their locality. Just over 1 in 3 churches were linked in this way – allowing for the overlap where people have described Churches Together as their 'local Council of Churches'. The number linked in this way has risen substantially from the 1988 figure of 18%.

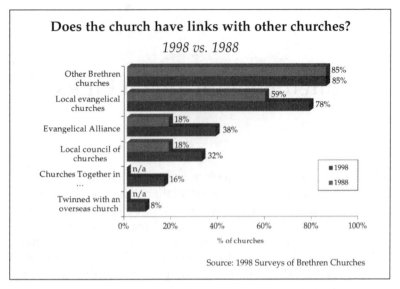

Chart 64: Links with other churches and associations

It is increasingly common for there to be links with churches in countries overseas. Eight per cent of churches were linked in this way.

It was more common for the larger churches to have developed the links we asked about. This may reflect a greater openness, a realisation of the benefits of relationships with other bodies and churches of all sorts or perhaps just that they had the ability and willingness to devote the time to working on rela-

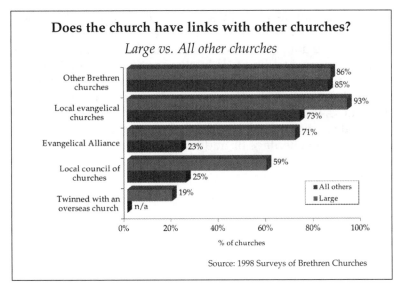

Does the church have links with other churches?

Large vs. All other churches

Source: 1998 Surveys of Brethren Churches

tionships with others.

Chart 65: Links with other Churches and Associations – Large vs Other

Size is not a factor in links with other Brethren churches. The gap widens somewhat for links with other evangelical churches. For links beyond that the gap grows very wide. Large churches have been the most energetic in twinning with churches in other countries.

Summary and Conclusions

Brethren churches have been sturdy advocates of autonomy for generations, have fiercely resisted claims that they were part of a denomination, yet have developed links over the years with other churches they recognised as Brethren. This reflects the importance of non-denominationalism and the unity of the (invisible) universal church in traditional Brethren thinking of the Open variety, at least in many parts of Britain. Some people have seen a decline in the strength of these 'invisible' bonds, yet many churches do seem to still have ties with other Brethren churches. In the past there has been a reluctance among many of the assemblies to become involved with other Evangelical churches locally, let alone those other churches, judged to be less than biblical in their beliefs and practice – by Brethren standards anyway. The data indicates that much of this reluctance is being whittled away. No doubt, as in other areas of life, Brethren are discovering that what they came to believe was anathema, has seemed on closer inspection to have much to commend it. Doubtless, too, they are finding that there is something to learn from other Christians, who own Christ as Lord, yet do not have quite the same heritage or traditions.